SOCIAL
MEDIA
SENSATIONS

Pinterest

Jill C. Wheeler

**Checkerboard
Library**

An Imprint of Abdo Publishing
abdopublishing.com

abdopublishing.com

Published by Abdo Publishing, a division of ABDO, PO Box 398166, Minneapolis, Minnesota 55439. Copyright © 2017 by Abdo Consulting Group, Inc. International copyrights reserved in all countries. No part of this book may be reproduced in any form without written permission from the publisher. Checkerboard Library™ is a trademark and logo of Abdo Publishing.

Printed in the United States of America, North Mankato, Minnesota
062016
092016

Design: Emily Love, Mighty Media, Inc.
Production: Mighty Media, Inc.
Editor: Liz Salzmann
Cover Photos: Shutterstock
Interior Photos: AP Images, pp. 5, 13, 17, 19; Conor McCabe Photography, p. 5;
Getty Images, p. 5; iStockphoto, pp. 9, 23, 27; Shutterstock, pp. 4, 6, 7, 11, 15, 21, 25, 29

Publishers Cataloging-in-Publication Data
Names: Wheeler, Jill C., author.
Title: Pinterest / by Jill C. Wheeler.
Description: Minneapolis, MN : Abdo Publishing, [2017] | Series: Social media
    sensations | Includes index.
Identifiers: LCCN 2016934275 | ISBN 9781680781915 (lib. bdg.) |
    ISBN 9781680775761 (ebook)
Subjects: LCSH: Pinterest--Juvenile literature. | Internet marketing--Juvenile
    literature. | Photography--Digital techniques--Juvenile literature. | Internet
    industry--United States--Juvenile literature. | Online social networks--Juvenile
    literature.
 Classification: DDC 658.872--dc23
LC record available at /http://lccn.loc.gov/2016934275

Contents

	Social Media Profile	4
	Meet the Founders	5
Chapter 1	What Is Pinterest?	6
Chapter 2	Online Collections	8
Chapter 3	Early Appeal	10
Chapter 4	Keeping It Going	12
Chapter 5	Growing Fast	14
Chapter 6	Nice People Wanted	16
Chapter 7	Business Connections	18
Chapter 8	Making a Difference	20
Chapter 9	Safety Online	22
Chapter 10	Life More Creative	24
Chapter 11	Pinterest's Future	26
	A Guide to Pinterest	28
	Glossary	30
	Websites	31
	Index	32

Pinterest

URL: http://www.pinterest.com

PURPOSE: Pinterest is a website for creating collections of images and information found on the Internet.

CURRENT CEO: Ben Silbermann

NUMBER OF USERS:
More than 100 million

NOVEMBER 2009
Silbermann gets the idea for Pinterest

MARCH 2010
Date of launch

MARCH 2011
Pinterest is released as an iPhone app

JUNE 2015
Buyable pins are introduced

Meet the Founders

BEN SILBERMANN was born in Des Moines, Iowa. He attended Yale University in New Haven, Connecticut. After Silbermann graduated in 2003, he worked at Google. He left Google in 2008 and founded Pinterest with Paul Sciarra and Evan Sharp.

PAUL SCIARRA attended Yale University, where he met Silbermann. He worked with Silbermann and Sharp to create Pinterest. Sciarra was the CEO until he left the company in 2012.

EVAN SHARP grew up in York, Pennsylvania. He met Silbermann through a mutual friend. Silbermann asked Sharp to help develop Pinterest. Sharp is the company's Chief Creative Officer.

Paul Sciarra

Ben Silbermann

Evan Sharp

CHAPTER 1

What Is Pinterest?

You just got a great new shirt. But you're not sure what to wear with it. Pinterest can help! You type a description of the shirt into the search box with the word "outfits." You hit enter. Suddenly, you see images of many ways other people are wearing a shirt similar to yours. In fact, one of the images includes other pieces similar to ones you already own. Now you have ideas for putting together a great new outfit! Welcome to Pinterest.

Pinterest can help you make a fashion statement!

Pinterest users can create a board of recipes they would like to try.

Pinterest users create boards on different topics. Then they pin images and articles from other websites or Pinterest pages to the boards. The pins form **grids** on the boards. Each pin has a link to the item's original location.

Pinterest users can make boards secret or public. A secret board can only be seen by its creator. A public board can be seen by other Pinterest users.

Pinterest inspires users to create, discover, and explore. This site is useful for planning events or learning hobbies. Users find ideas for crafts, vacations, recipes, and more.

CHAPTER 2

Online Collections

Pinterest was founded by three men. Ben Silbermann is the main person behind Pinterest. He worked with Paul Sciarra and Evan Sharp to create the website.

Silbermann and Sciarra had worked together before. In 2008, they started a company called Cold Brew Labs. The company's first project was an app called Tote. It let people look at online catalogs on their phones. However, few people used this app.

Then Silbermann got another idea. As a child, he liked to collect objects and display his collections. He wanted to create a way to something similar online. In November 2009, he and Sciarra started working on Pinterest.

Around this time, Silbermann met Sharp. Silbermann told Sharp about Pinterest. Sharp designed the website. He created more than 50 versions before the team settled on one. Finally, in March 2010, Cold Brew Labs launched Pinterest!

Silbermann collected insects as a kid. The Pinterest board idea came from pinning insects to a board.

CHAPTER 3

Early Appeal

The founders first sent Pinterest to **colleagues**, friends, and family members. New users had to be invited to join by current Pinterest users. This meant Pinterest did not grow very quickly. But the site slowly started to catch on.

One thing some Pinterest users, or pinners, found appealing was that they didn't have to create their own content. Not everyone wants to write original **tweets** or Facebook posts. Pinterest offers people another way to share content that interests them.

Instead of writing posts, Pinterest users search for content on the Internet. Popular search topics include home improvement, fashion, pets, and more. Then users pin links to content they find to their boards.

Did You Know?

Most Pinterest pins are photos. But users can also pin video and audio files!

Pinterest helps people with similar interests connect with each other. Users can follow other pinners. Then they are notified if someone they are following adds a pin. Users can also invite friends to follow their boards. And people can comment on each other's pins and boards.

Boards can also be used to **collaborate** on a project or event. A user can invite one or more pinners to work on a board together. Each collaborator can add pins to the board.

Pinning

Users can post content to Pinterest in many ways. To create a new pin, a Pinner **uploads** an image. Pinners also repin each other's posts.

Pinners can also pin content from websites. Many **online** images have "Pin it" buttons. Clicking these buttons lets users pin the images to their boards.

There is also a Pinterest browser button users can install. It appears as a Pinterest logo on the browser toolbar. A user clicks this button while online. This highlights images from the page that the user can pin.

CHAPTER 4

Keeping It Going

Pinterest needed more than just a lot of users in order to succeed. It also needed money. The company has to pay for office space. It has to pay the salaries of its employees, who keep the site running. Computers and other necessary equipment also cost money.

Pinterest doesn't charge people to use the site, so it has to get funding from investors. Investors give money to companies that they think will be successful. Then the companies pay the investors back if they do well.

At first, Pinterest had trouble attracting investors. People didn't understand the website. So, they didn't think it would be worth investing in.

Then, in May 2010, an investor told the founders she loved Pinterest and wanted to invest in it. Soon, other investors followed. Over the next two years, Pinterest received more than $100 million in investment funding.

Pinterest used some of the money for new office space. The company was outgrowing its small office in Palo Alto, California. In July 2012, Pinterest moved its headquarters to a building in San Francisco, California. The company also has offices in nine other cities around the world.

CHAPTER 5

Growing Fast

Pinterest continued to become more popular throughout 2010. At the end of that year, it had 10,000 users. By July 2013, the number of Pinterest users reached 70 million. Several changes during these years helped Pinterest grow.

In 2011, Pinterest released its iPhone app. Then, in 2012, apps for iPad and Android came out. These apps allowed pinners to use Pinterest on **mobile** devices. Users could create and view pins wherever they went.

Another change made it easier to become a Pinterest member. Starting in August 2012, people no longer needed to be invited to join Pinterest. They could just go to the website or **download** the app and create accounts.

Pinterest also received some good publicity during its early years. It was included in *Time* magazine's list of "50 Websites That Make the Web Great" in August 2011. And celebrities started using Pinterest. Famous pinners

include singer Katy Perry, reality TV star Andrew Zimmern, and talk show host Ellen DeGeneres. This publicity and celebrity interest helped increase Pinterest's popularity.

CHAPTER 6

Nice People Wanted

Funding is important for Pinterest's success. However, Pinterest's founders say other factors are also important. They focus on building a team that works well together. Sharp says they "try to hire people who are 'nice.'"

One example of Pinterest's team-building is KnitCon. *Knit* is how Pinterest employees describe their work **environment**. It refers to being able to see one another's point of view. This helps people with different jobs understand each other. So, engineers, marketers, and designers can work together better.

Being knit also means trying new things and having interests outside of work. Pinterest encourages its employees to do this with a yearly KnitCon event. *Con* is short for **convention**. During KnitCon, employees teach each other fun hobbies or useful skills. KnitCon topics have included fixing bicycles, making **sushi**, and solving crossword puzzles.

Pinterest employees unwind during breaks by playing foosball.

Pinterest is also focused on **diversity**. In 2015, the company announced a goal of having women make up 30 percent of its engineers. Pinterest also set a goal of hiring more people of color.

CHAPTER 7

Business Connections

Pinterest helps people discover things they did not know they were looking for. It has spurred millions of people to try new activities. These include everything from building projects to travel adventures and hobbies.

Often, trying new things can mean spending money. Pinterest fits well with business because users often pin items that people can buy. So, when someone clicks on these pins, they are taken to the sellers' websites.

Companies have started using Pinterest to attract customers directly. Businesses create boards to showcase their products, events, and services. Companies can see how popular their products are by how often pins featuring those products are looked at and shared.

In 2015, Pinterest introduced buyable pins. Now users could buy certain items on boards through Pinterest. This made doing business on the site even easier.

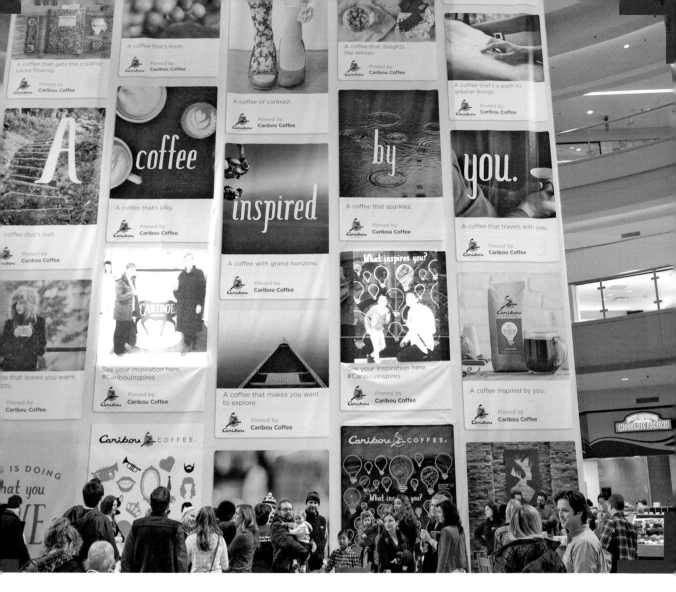

In 2014, coffee chain Caribou installed a huge Pinterest board at the Mall of America in Bloomington, Minnesota. This was to celebrate the launch of a coffee blend created using ideas from the company's Pinterest followers.

CHAPTER 8

Making a Difference

Pinterest isn't only for collecting images or selling products. Pinterest has also helped with social awareness. These efforts raise support for important causes.

Starting in 2011, the American Heart Association has included Pinterest in its Go Red for Women campaign. The campaign's goal is to raise awareness of how heart disease affects women. Each February, the campaign asks people to pin images featuring the color red.

Another campaign that used Pinterest was #AcceptanceMatters. It was created by MasterCard in 2013. The company's message was that people should accept one another. MasterCard asked pinners to create pins related to acceptance. People responded with thousands of pins about kindness, love, and tolerance.

Macy's annual Go Red for Women fashion show. The store makes a contribution for each Pinterest pin tagged #MacysGoesRed.

CHAPTER 9

Safety Online

With campaigns, business pages, crafts, celebrities, and more, Pinterest draws all types of users. The site works to remove **inappropriate** content. However, using any social-**networking** site can have safety risks. It is important users post and interact on these sites safely.

Scams can be found on Pinterest. These often involve pins offering prizes. Clicking on these pins directs users to other websites. There, they may be asked to share personal information or **download** files. It's important users only click on links they know are trustworthy.

Another scam invites users to **collaborate** on a board. The only problem is that board is fake. The creator just wants to get personal information from other users. Users should only collaborate with others they know and trust.

It is important to use social media sites safely. A trusted adult can help younger users navigate these sites.

CHAPTER 10

Life More Creative

Pinterest is currently working to make the site more international. Pinterest is already **available** in more than 30 languages. Focus areas for the future include Europe, Japan, and Brazil. Pinterest also hopes to make the site more interactive. Recent changes allow users to **download** apps from within Pinterest.

People keep finding new ways to use Pinterest. Some teachers are using boards to plan lessons or share materials. Other people use Pinterest to share funny Internet **memes**. Still others find that Pinterest remains a great way to search for creative ideas.

Pinterest's founders believe many everyday activities involve creativity. These include working at a job, raising a child, and going to school. Pinterest aims to help users recognize this and insert more creativity into their lives. Users are inspired by the site's millions of creative dreams.

Seventy percent of Pinterest users planned their wedding on the site before they were even engaged!

There are dreams of new recipes, dreams of weddings, and dreams of fun projects. Whatever can be imagined, Pinterest users can pin it!

CHAPTER 11

Pinterest's Future

Pinterest is not the only company focused on inspiring creativity. It has faced competition in recent years. In 2015, Internet giant Google introduced Collections. It is a Google+ site feature that is similar to Pinterest.

Despite competition, Pinterest is confident it can stay on top. Its team continues working to make the site more interesting and useful. Pinterest has remained useful for business. Contests have become popular ways for companies to interact with buyers. Many offer pinners a chance to win products or prizes in return for repins.

Whatever the future looks like for Pinterest, its users are sure to shape it. Pinners will continue to share, inspire, and explore. And their creativity will be captured on boards for the world to see!

Pinterest encourages pinners to pin their real-world interests and then get out and enjoy them!

Pinterest

Pinterest users must be at least 13 to have an account. To start pinning, users visit www.pinterest.com. Then, they enter an e-mail address and a **password** to sign up.

Many other websites are linked to Pinterest through "Pin it" or "P" buttons. These buttons make pinning easy. Clicking them takes users to their Pinterest account. Then they choose a board they want to pin the content to.

Users can add pins by clicking "Add a pin" from one of their boards. Next, they choose an image from a website or from their computer. Pinterest's search feature lets pinners search other users' boards for pins too. Users can repin this content with one click.

Users can follow other pinners' boards that they like. This is done by clicking "Follow board" on that user's board. Then, the user will see any new pins posted to that board.